T0088927

Sensual Love Poems

Sensual Love Poems

COLLECTED BY

KATHLEEN BLEASE

Ballantine Books • New York

TO MY LOVE,

Roger

A Ballantine Book
Published by The Random House Publishing Group

Introduction and compilation copyright © 2002 by The Random House Publishing Group, a division of Random House, Inc.

Published in the United States by Ballantine Books, an imprint of The Random House Publishing Group, a division of Random House, Inc., New York, and simultaneously in Canada by Random House of Canada Limited, Toronto.

Ballantine and colophon are trademarks of Random House, Inc.

www.ballantinebooks.com

Library of Congress Cataloging-in-Publication Data is available upon request from the publisher.

ISBN 0-345-44787-5

First Edition: January 2002

147028622

CONTENTS

❊

II
A Love Like Mine

III
Reflections of Love

ACKNOWLEDGMENTS

Though poets of past and present are responsible for these remarkable verses, this collection required the talents and considerations of others. My editor, Patricia Peters, provided guidance and patience, while production editors, copyeditors, designers, and managers all had a hand in this book's wonderful appeal. I am thankful for all their efforts. As usual, my family showed understanding and, once again, allowed me free time to complete my work. So to Ben, Max, and Roger, many hugs and kisses for the kindness and loving encouragement you dished out.

INTRODUCTION

❀

Falling in love makes the senses work as they were meant to work! There is a surprising freshness to the world, like a newborn taking her first breath and feeling her mother's touch for the first time. To someone in love, the air itself suddenly has a distinctive aroma. The breeze through the trees sings a song. Rain makes a tranquilizing cadence.

Indeed, true love's effects are fascinating. In this new titillative life, it reshapes the world for two lovers and makes their little corner seem like a mountaintop—it is soaring, refreshing, colorful, soothing. It can ring or shout. It can tingle or warm. It can make you talkative or observant and silent, whichever is *not* like your character. Love makes you want to know all that is around you. Common everyday things, things that have *always* been around, are now endearing images seared into the heart. Love even alters time. It manages to slow the clock while it gracefully blends yesterday into tomorrow.

What remarkable alterations love makes to a life's pattern!

And what would a new life be without its own language? Love indeed has its own language, a sensual code. Twirling a lover's hair around a finger, a kiss on the neck, a gentle touch when walking by, a long, smothering embrace, a glance across a room: each an expression of a magical connection. This is the basic element of a lifelong romance.

Perhaps more than anyone, poets are destined to decode the sensual language of love, as they are dedicated to the essence of the words—their textures, tempos, imageries, timbre, and the mysterious ways they can call upon the senses, stir them, and rearrange them into a new perspective. Like being in love!

Shakespeare, Donne, Wordsworth, Teasdale, Rossetti, Barrett Browning, Puccini, Gerald Stern, W. S. Merwin, and Maya Angelou are but a few of the poets you will find in *Sensual Love Poems*. Between these covers are some of literature's most sensual creations. Enjoy.

Kathleen Blease
Easton, Pennsylvania

I

Awakenings
of Love

ANCIENT EGYPTIAN LOVE LYRIC

❀

Your love has gone all through my body
like honey in water,
as a drug is mixed into spices,
as water is mingled with wine.
Oh that you would speed to see your sister
like a charger on the battlefield, like a bull to his
        pasture!
For the heavens are sending us love like a flame
        spreading through straw
and desire like the swoop of the falcon!

ANONYMOUS
[C. 1085–C. 570 B.C.]

———

FLOWER OF LOVE

The perfume of your body dulls my sense.
I want nor wine nor weed; your breath alone
Suffices. In this moment rare and tense
I worship at your breast. The flower is blown
The saffron petals tempt my amorous mouth,
The yellow heart is radiant now with dew
Soft-scented, redolent of my loved South;
O flower of love! I give myself to you.
Uncovered on your couch of figured green,
Here let us linger indivisible.
The portals of your sanctuary unseen
Receive my offering, yielding unto me.
Oh, with our love the night is warm and deep!
The air is sweet, my flower, and sweet the flute
Whose music lulls our burning brain to sleep,
While we lie loving, passionate and mute.

CLAUDE McKAY
[1890–1948]

THE BAIT

Come live with me, and be my love,
And we will some new pleasures prove
Of golden sands, and crystal brooks,
With silken lines, and silver hooks.

There will the river whispering run
Warmed by thy eyes, more than the sun.
And there the' enamoured fish will stay,
Begging themselves they may betray.

When thou wilt swim in that live bath,
Each fish, which every channel hath,
Will amorously to thee swim,
Gladder to catch thee, than thou him.

If thou, to be so seen, be'st loth,
By sun, or moon, thou darkenest both,
And if myself have leave to see,
I need not their light, having thee.

Let others freeze with angling reeds,
And cut their legs, with shells and weeds,
Or treacherously poor fish beset,
With strangling snare, or windowy net:

Let coarse bold hands, from slimy nest
The bedded fish in banks out-wrest,
Of curious traitors, sleavesilk flies
Bewitch poor fishes' wandering eyes.

For thee, thou need'st no such deceit,
For thou thyself art thine own bait,
That fish, that is not catched thereby,
Alas, is wiser far than I.

JOHN DONNE
[1572–1631]

SO JUST KISS ME

So just kiss me and let my hair
messy itself in your fingers

tell me nothing needs to be done—
no clocks need winding

There is no bell without a voice
needing to borrow my own

instead, let me steady myself
in the arms

of a man who won't ask me to be
what he needs, but lets me exist

as I am

   a blonde flame
   a hurricane

wrapped up
in a tiny body

that will come to his arms
like the safest harbor

   for mending

JEWEL KILCHER
[1974–]

I LOVE YOU

I love your lips when they're wet with wine
And red with a wild desire;
I love your eyes when the lovelight lies
Lit with a passionate fire.
I love your arms when the warm white flesh
Touches mine in a fond embrace;
I love your hair when the strands enmesh
Your kisses against my face.

Not for me the cold calm kiss
Of a virgin's bloodless love;
Not for me the saint's white bliss,
Nor the heart of a spotless dove.
But give me the love that so freely gives
And laughs at the whole world's blame,
With your body so young and warm in my arms,
It sets my poor heart aflame.

So kiss me sweet with your warm wet mouth,
Still fragrant with ruby wine,
And say with a fervor born of the South
That your body and soul are mine.
Clasp me close in your warm young arms,
While the pale stars shine above,
And we'll live our whole young lives away
In the joys of a living love.

ELLA WHEELER WILCOX
[1850–1919]

9

SONNET XXXVIII

First time he kissed me, he but only kissed
The finger of this hand wherewith I write;
And ever since, it grew more clean and white,
Slow to world-greetings, quick with its "Oh, list,"
When the angels speak. A ring of amethyst
I could not wear here, plainer to my sight,
Than that first kiss. The second passed in height
The first, and sought the forehead, and half missed,
Half falling on the hair. O beyond meed!
That was the chrism of love, which love's own crown,
With sanctifying sweetness, did precede.
The third upon my lips was folded down
In perfect, purple state; since when, indeed,
I have been proud and said, "My love, my own."

ELIZABETH BARRETT BROWNING
[1806–1861]

THE KISS

*B*efore you kissed me only winds of heaven
Had kissed me, and the tenderness of rain—
Now you have come, how can I care for kisses
Like theirs again?

I sought the sea, she sent her winds to meet me,
They surged about me singing of the south—
I turned my head away to keep still holy
Your kiss upon my mouth.

And swift sweet rains of shining April weather
Found not my lips where living kisses are;
I bowed my head lest they put out my glory
As rain puts out a star.

I am my love's and he is mine forever,
Sealed with a seal and safe forevermore—
Think you that I could let a beggar enter
Where a king stood before?

SARA TEASDALE
[1884–1933]

MIA BUTTERFLY
from opera *MADAME BUTTERFLY*

PINKERTON

   Give me you hands, I'll cover them with kisses!
      (bursts out very tenderly)
   My Butterfly!—How very well they named you,
   Tender, fragile creature!—

BUTTERFLY *(at these words her face clouds over and she*
      draws away her hands)

   There across the ocean, when butterflies are caught,
   I've often heard it is the custom to impale them—
   Then on cardboard to nail them!

PINKERTON *(gently taking her hands again and smiling)*

   That's true, I can't deny,
   But shall I tell you why?—
   So they can't fly away!
      (embracing her)
   And I have caught you, and so I want to hold you.
   Be mine now!

BUTTERFLY

   Now and forever.
      (throwing herself in his arms)

GIACOMO PUCCINI
[1858–1924]

12

LAUS VENERIS (EXCERPT)

Fair still, but fair for no man saving me,
As when she came out of the naked sea
Making the foam as fire whereon she trod,
And as the inner flower of fire was she.

Yea, she laid hold upon me, and her mouth
Clove unto mine as soul to body doth,
And, laughing, made her lips luxurious;
Her hair had smells of all the sunburnt south,

Strange spice and flower, strange savour of crushed
        fruit,
And perfume the swart kings tread underfoot
For pleasure when their minds wax amorous,
Charred frankincense and grated sandal-root.

And I forgot fear and all weary things,
All ended prayers and perished thanksgivings,
Feeling her face with all her eager hair
Cleave to me, clinging as a fire that clings

To the body and to the raiment, burning them;
As after death I know that such-like flame
Shall cleave to me for ever; yea, what care,
Albeit I burn then, having felt the same?

Ah love, there is no better life than this;
To have known love, how bitter a thing it is,
And afterward be cast out of God's sight;
Yea, these that know not, shall they have such bliss

High up in barren heaven before his face
As we twain in the heavy-hearted place,
Remembering love and all the dead delight,
And all that time was sweet with for a space?

For till the thunder in the trumpet be,
Soul may divide from body, but not we
One from another; I hold thee with my hand,
I let mine eyes have all their will of thee,
I seal myself upon thee with my might,
Abiding alway out of all men's sight
Until God loosen over sea and land
The thunder of the trumpets of the night.

ALGERNON CHARLES SWINBURNE
[1837–1909]

ON A GIRDLE

That which her slender waist confin'd,
Shall now my joyful temples bind;
No monarch but would give his crown,
His arms might do what this has done.

It was my heaven's extremest sphere,
The pale which held that lovely deer,
My joy, my grief, my hope, my love,
Did all within this circle move.

A narrow compass, and yet there
Dwelt all that's good, and all that's fair;
Give me but what this ribbon bound,
Take all the rest the sun goes round.

EDMUND WALLER
[1606–1687]

THE MORNING

The first morning
I woke in surprise to your body
for I had been dreaming it
as I do

all around us white petals had never slept
leaves touched the early light
your breath warm as your skin on my neck
your eyes opening

smell of dew

W. S. MERWIN
[1927–]

MADONNA OF THE EVENING FLOWERS

All day long I have been working,
Now I am tired.
I call: "Where are you?"
But there is only the oak tree rustling in the wind.
The house is very quiet,
The sun shines in on your books,
On your scissors and thimble just put down,
But you are not there.
Suddenly I am lonely:
Where are you?
I go about searching.

Then I see you,
Standing under a spire of pale blue larkspur,
With a basket of roses on your arm.
You are cool, like silver,
And you smile.
I think the Canterbury bells are playing little tunes,
You tell me that the peonies need spraying,
That the columbines have overrun all bounds,
That the pyrus japonica should be cut back and
          rounded.

You tell me these things.
But I look at you, heart of silver,
White heart-flame of polished silver,
Burning beneath the blue steeples of the larkspur,
And I long to kneel instantly at your feet,
While all about us peal the loud,
sweet *Te Deums* of the Canterbury bells.

AMY LOWELL

[1874–1925]

COLLECT BEADS OF NIGHT

Collect beads of night
Fill your
skin with the dark weight of the
wet sky. Let boldness live in your heart
and I will recognize you
amongst the many
and claim you
as my own

JEWEL KILCHER
[1974–]

19

TO CYNTHIA
On concealment of her beauty

$\mathcal{D}$o not conceale thy radiant eyes,
The starre-light of serenest skies,
Least wanting of their heavenly light,
They turne to *Chaos* endlesse night.

Do not conceale those tresses faire,
The silken snares of thy curl'd haire,
Least finding neither gold, nor Ore,
The curious Silke-worme worke no more.

Do not conceale those brests of thine,
More snowe white then the Apenine,
Least if there be like cold or frost,
The Lilly be for ever lost.

Do not conceale that fragrant scent,
Thy breath, which to all flowers hath lent
Perfumes, least it being supprest,
No spices growe in all the East.

Do not conceale thy heavenly voice,
Which makes the hearts of gods rejoyce,
Least Musicke hearing no such thing,
The Nightingale forget to sing.

Do not conceale, not yet eclipse
Thy pearly teeth with Corrall lips,
Least that the Seas cease to bring forth
Gems, which from thee have all their worth.

Do not conceale no beauty grace,
That's either in thy minde or face,
Least vertue overcome by vice,
Make men beleeve no Paradice.

SIR FRANCIS KYNASTON
[1587–1642]

A BRIDAL SONG

She is more sparkling beautiful
Than dawn-light seen thro' tears
The weeping worlds of Paradise
Shed down upon the spheres.

Her eyes are bright and passionate
With love's immortal flame—
The flowers of a wildwood tree
In petals write her name.

Her breath of life's so wondrous sweet
The bees halt, in amaze,
Their streaming honey-laden fleet
Above the meadow ways;

And every little singing thing
Atween the breasted hill
And God's high-vaulted cloistering
Upraises with a will

Paeans of laud, and cheery chaunts
Of her, who now is mine—
Queen-Angel of angelic haunts
Thro' months of mead and wine.

HUGH MCCRAE
[1876–1958]

JUNE FIRST
For Abigail Thomas

*S*ome blossoms are so white and luscious, when they
hold their long thin hands up you strip them for love
and scatter them on the ground as you walk;

and some birds look at you as if there were no
great line drawn between their lives and yours,
as if you drank together from the same cement;

and some pods spin in the wind as if you would not
      pick
them up gingerly to see if they had wings
and then would not break them open to see what
      made them
fall, to study their visceras.

I touch you as I would the sawdust in the eaves
or the crazy buttercups in the middle of the mulepath
or the frightening foil
jumping and leaping in front of the oily grackles;

and I touch you as I touch the grass, my body falls
        down on the ground
and I pull at the roots as I watch you in the limbs
bending down to avoid the red blossoms,
hiding in the leaves,
reaching up like the tallest dryad,
your curved arms and your jeweled fingers
waving slowly again in the hot sun.

GERALD STERN
[1925–]

SUMMER DOORWAY

❁

I come down from the gold mountains
each of them the light of many years
high up the soughing of cold pines among stones
the whole way home dry grass seething
to these sounds I think of you already there
in the house all my steps lead to

you have the table set to surprise me
you are lighting the two candles

W. S. MERWIN
[1927-]

LOVE POEM

We made love last night
beneath the stars.
The moon's Cycloptic eye
unblinking
staring us down
uncovering our bodies of the darkness
like naked roots
we tangled ourselves
thighs and elbows heavy fruit
shiny as winter chestnuts.
Body of the man I love—
bitten mouth, tangerine lips
rose petal surprise of tongue,
I could wander the continent
of your golden valleys
without ceasing
and delight each day
in discovering
a new dawn
rising from the depths
of your mysterious being.

JEWEL KILCHER
[1974–]

GREY-EYED MABEL

I gazed on orbs of flashing black;
I met the glow of hazel light;
I marked the hue of laughing blue,
That sparkled in the festive night.
But none could fling a lasting spell
To hold me with unchanging power—
The chains they cast were never fast
Beyond the gay and fleeting hour—
Till Grey-eyed Mabel's gentle glance,
With blushing sense and beauty rife,
Bade my soul cry with burning sigh,
"I'm thine, and only thine, for life."
Black, blue, and hazel stars have set,
But Mabel's grey eyes lead me yet.

What was it in sweet Mabel's eyes
That told me what no others told,
That roused the dull, that pleased the wise,
That charmed the young and cheered the old?
What was it held my world-worn breast
In holy thrall—unknown before?
What was it those grey eyes expressed
That made me worship and adore?
It was the pure and tender ray
That filled those eyes in joy or woe;
It was the beam that could not play
Without the fountain stream below;

It was the beam of simple truth,
Of Woman's faith and trusting Youth.

Those soft, grey eyes were watched by mine
With earnest, deep, and secret prayer;
I knew, I felt, my earthly shrine
Was found and fixed for ever—there.
I poured my heart one moonlit night
Into sweet Mabel's listening ear;
Our mutual vow, from then till now,
Bound each to each—fond, firm, and dear.
Our boys and girls are growing round,
And all give promise, brave and fair,
But one young cherub form is found
First in my love, my hope, my care.
And why?—ah! why? My soul replies,
"She has dear Mabel's soft, grey eyes."

ELIZA COOK
[1818–1889]

ROMANCE

To clasp you now and feel your head close-pressed,
Scented and warm against my beating breast;
To whisper soft and quivering your name,
And drink the passion burning in your frame;
To lie at full length, taut, with cheek to cheek,
And tease your mouth with kisses till you speak
Love words, mad words, dream words, sweet senseless
        words,
Melodious like notes of mating birds;
To hear you ask if I shall love always,
And myself answer: Till the end of days;
To feel your easeful sigh of happiness
When on your trembling lips I murmur: Yes;
It is so sweet. We know it is not true.
What matters it! The night must shed her dew.
We know it is not true, but it is sweet—
The poem with this music is complete.

CLAUDE McKAY
[1890–1948]

29

EROS (EXCERPT)

(II)

y mouth is wet with your life,
my eyes blinded with your face,
a heart itself which feels
the intimate music.

My mind is caught,
dimmed with it,
(where is love taking us?)
my lips are wet with your life.

In my body were pearls cast,
shot with Ionian tints, purple,
vivid through the white.

HILDA DOOLITTLE
[1886–1961]

FOR THE COURTESAN CH'ING LIN

On your slender body
Your jade and coral girdle ornaments chime
Like those of a celestial companion
Come from the Green Jade City of Heaven.
One smile from you when we meet,
And I become speechless and forget every word.
For too long you have gathered flowers,
And leaned against the bamboos,
Your green sleeves growing cold,
In your deserted valley:
I can visualize you all alone,
A girl harboring her cryptic thoughts.

You glow like a perfumed lamp
In the gathering shadows.
We play wine games
And recite each other's poems.
Then you sing "Remembering South of the River"
With its heart breaking verses. Then
We paint each other's beautiful eyebrows.
I want to possess you completely
Your jade body
And your promised heart.
It is Spring.
Vast mists cover the Five Lakes.
My dear, let me buy a red painted boat
And carry you away.

WU TSAO
[C. 1800–?]

E LUCEVAN LE STELLE
(*"AND THE STARS WERE SHINING"*)
from opera *Tosca*

*A*nd the stars were shining . . .
The earth smelt sweet . . .
The garden gate creaked . . .
And a footstep brushed the sand.
She entered, fragrant,
And fell into my arms.
O soft kisses, tender caresses,
While I, all a-quiver,
Unveiled her lovely features!
Vanished for ever is my dream of love . . .
That time has fled
And I die in despair.
Never have I loved life so dearly!

GIACOMO PUCCINI
[1858–1924]

SONG

𝓘t was as if she had brought the cooling rain,
the breeze through the curtained window,
the taste of the bourbon,
so that I turned to the street again,
happy in the traffic and the rain.

HARVEY SHAPIRO
[1924–]

CELESTE AIDA, FORMA DIVINA
("HEAVENLY AIDA, WONDERFUL MAIDEN")
from opera *Aida*

Heavenly Aida, wonderful maiden,
Mystical garland, bright as a flower,
With love for your beauty my life is laden,
Over my spirit I feel your power.
Would I could set your fair skies around you,
Gather you breezes when day is done.
How I would gladly with gold have crowned you,
Built you a throne near the shining sun!

GIUSEPPE VERDI
[1813–1901]

LOVE IN THE VALLEY (EXCERPTS)

*U*nder yonder beech-tree single on the green-sward,
Couched with her arms behind her golden head,
Knees and tresses folded to slip and ripple idly,
Lies my young love sleeping in the shade.
Had I the heart to slide an arm beneath her,
Press her parting lips as her waist I gather slow,
Waking in amazement she could not but embrace me:
Then would she hold me and never let me go?

Shy as the squirrel and wayward as the swallow,
Swift as the swallow along the river's light
Circleting the surface to meet his mirrored winglets,
Fleeter she seems in her stay than in her flight.
Shy as the squirrel that leaps among the pine-tops,
Wayward as the swallow overhead at set of sun,
She whom I love is hard to catch and conquer,
Hard, but O the glory of the winning were she won!

When her mother tends her before the laughing
            mirror,
Tying up her laces, looping up her hair,
Often she thinks, were this wild thing wedded,
More love should I have, and much less care.
When her mother tends her before the lighted mirror,
Loosening her laces, combing down her curls,
Often she thinks, were this wild thing wedded,
I should miss but one for many boys and girls.

. . . .

When at dawn she sighs, and like an infant to the
      window
Turns grave eyes craving light, released from dreams,
Beautiful she looks, like a white water-lily
Bursting out of bud in havens of the streams.
When from bed she rises clothed from neck to ankle
In her long nightgown sweet as boughs of May,
Beautiful she looks, like a tall garden lily
Pure from the night, and splendid for the day.

. . . .

Hither she comes; she comes to me; she lingers,
Deepens her brown eyebrows, while in new surprise
High rise the lashes in wonder of a stranger;
Yet am I the light and living of her eyes.
Something friends have told her fills her heart to
      brimming,
Nets her in her blushes, and wounds her, and tames.—
Sure of her haven, O like a dove alighting,
Arms up, she dropped: our souls were in our names.

GEORGE MEREDITH
[1828–1909]

———

37

A TRYST IN THE SPRING
SONG OF SONGS 2:8–17

*H*ark! My lover—here he comes
Springing across the mountains,
Leaping across the hills.

My lover is like a gazelle
Or a young stag.
Here he stands behind our wall,
Gazing through the windows,
Peering through the lattices.

My lover speaks: he says to me,
"Arise, my beloved, my beautiful one, and come!
"For see, the winter is past,
the rains are over and gone.
The flowers appear on the earth,
The time of the pruning the vines has come,
And the song of the dove is heard in our land.

The fig tree puts forth its figs,
And the vines, in bloom, give forth fragrance.
Arise, my beloved, my beautiful one, and come!

"O my dove in the clefts of the rock,
in the secret recesses of the cliff,
Let me see you,
Let me hear your voice,
For your voice is sweet,
And you are lovely."

Catch us the foxes, the little foxes
That damage the vineyards;
For our vineyards are in bloom!

My lover belongs to me and I to him;
He browses among the lillies.
Until the day breathes cool and the
Shadows lengthen,
Roam, my lover,
Like a gazelle or a young stag
upon the mountains of Bether.

THE LOVER AND HIS GARDEN
SONG OF SONGS 4:12–16

*Y*ou are an enclosed garden, my sister, my bride,
An enclosed garden, a fountain sealed.
You are a park that puts forth pomegranates,
With all choice fruits;
Nard and saffron, calamus and cinnamon,
With all kinds of incense;
Myrrh and aloes,
With all the finest spices.
You are a garden fountain, a well of water
Flowing fresh from Lebanon.
Arise, north wind? Come, south wind!
Blow upon my garden
That its perfumes may spread abroad.
Let my lover come to his garden and eat its choice
fruits.

JAN KUBELIK

*Y*our bow swept over a string, and a long low note
quivered to the air. (A mother of Bohemia sobs over a
      new child perfect
learning to suck milk.)

Your bow ran fast over all the high strings fluttering
and wild. (All the girls in Bohemia are laughing on a
      Sunday afternoon
in the hills with their lovers.)

CARL SANDBURG
[1878–1967]

LO, AS A CAREFUL HOUSEWIFE
RUNS TO CATCH

Lo, as a careful housewife runs to catch
One of her feathered creatures broke away,
Sets down her babe, and makes all swift dispatch
In pursuit of the thing she would have stay;
Whilst her neglected child holds her in chase,
Cries to catch her whose busy care is bent
To follow that which flies before her face,
Not prizing her poor infant's discontent:
So run'st thou after that which flies from thee,
Whilst I, thy babe, chase thee afar behind;
But if thou catch thy hope, turn back to me
And play the mother's part—kiss me, be kind.
   So will I pray that thou mayst have thy Will,
    If thou turn back and my loud crying still.

WILLIAM SHAKESPEARE
[1564–1616]

II

A Love
Like Mine

STARLIGHT

With two bright eyes, my star, my love,
Thou lookest on the stars above:
Ah, would that I the heaven might be
With a million eyes to look on thee.

PLATO
[C. 428–348 B.C.]

A RED FLOWER

Your lips are like a southern lily red,
Wet with soft rain-kisses of the night,
In which the brown bee buries deep its head,
When still the dawn's a silver sea of light.
Your lips betray the secret of your soul,
The dark delicious essence that is you,
A mystery of life, the flaming goal
I seek through mazy pathways strange and new.
Your lips are the red symbol of a dream.
What visions of warm lilies they impart,
That line the green bank of a fair blue stream,
With butterflies and bees close to each heart!
Brown bees that murmur sounds of music rare,
That softly fall upon the languorous breeze,
Wafting them gently on the quiet air
Among untended avenues of trees.
O were I hovering, a bee, to probe
Deep down within your scented heart, fair flower,
Enfolded by your soft vermilion robe,
Amorous of sweets, for but one perfect hour!

CLAUDE McKAY
[1890–1948]

46

36

*W*hen I am with you our loving
Won't let me sleep
Away from you the tears won't let me sleep.
God, it's amazing to be awake both nights,
But how different these awakenings are!

RUMI
[1207–1273]

AD FINUM

On the white throat of useless passion
That scorched my soul with its burning breath
I clutched my fingers in murderous fashion
And gathered them close in a grip of death;

For why should I fan, or feed with fuel,
A love that showed me but blank despair?
So my hold was firm, and my grasp was cruel—
I meant to strangle it then and there!

I thought it was dead. But, with no warning,
It rose from its grave last night and came
And stood by my bed till the early morning.
And over and over it spoke your name.

Its throat was red where my hands had held it;
It burned my brow with its scorching breath;
And I said, the moment my eyes beheld it,
"A love like this can know no death."

For just one kiss that your lips have given
In the lost and beautiful past to me,
I would gladly barter my hopes of Heaven
And all the bliss of Eternity.

For never a joy are the angels keeping,
To lay at my feet in Paradise,
Like that of into your strong arms creeping,
And looking into your love lit eyes.

I know, in the way that sins are reckoned,
This thought is a sin of the deepest dye;
But I know too that if an angel beckoned,
Standing close by the Throne on High,
And you, adown by the gates infernal,
Should open your loving arms and smile,
I would turn my back on things supernal,
To lie on your breast a little while.

To know for an hour you were mine completely—
Mine in body and soul, my own—
I would bear unending tortures sweetly,
With not a murmur and not a moan.

A lighter sin or lesser error
Might change through hope or fear divine;
But there is no fear, and hell hath no terror,
To change or alter a love like mine.

ELLA WHEELER WILCOX
[1850–1919]

GLOIRE DE DIJON

*W*hen she rises in the morning
I linger to watch her;
She spreads the bath-cloth underneath the window
And the sunbeams catch her
Glistening white on the shoulders,
While down her sides the mellow
Golden shadow glows as
She stoops to the sponge, and her swung breasts
Sway like full-blown yellow
Gloire de Dijon roses.

She drips herself with water, and her shoulders
Glisten as silver, they crumple up
Like wet and falling roses, and I listen
For the sluicing of their rain-dishevelled petals.
In the window full of sunlight
Concentrates her golden shadow
Fold on fold, until it glows as
Mellow as the glory roses.

DAVID HERBERT LAWRENCE
[1885–1930]

NESSUN DORMA
("NO MAN WILL SLEEP")
from opera *Turandot*

*N*o man will sleep! No man will sleep!
You, too, oh Princess,
In your virginal room,
Watch the stars
Trembling with love and hope!

But my secret lies hidden within me,
No-one shall discover my name!
Oh no, I will reveal it only on your lips
When daylight shines forth!
And my kiss shall break
The silence that makes you mine!

Depart, oh night! Set, you stars!
Set, you stars! At dawn I shall win!
I shall win! I shall win!

GIACOMO PUCCINI
[1858–1924]

LOVE'S DESIRES
SONG OF SONGS 1:2–4

❀

*L*et him kiss me with the kisses of his mouth!

More delightful is your love than wine!
Your name spoken is spreading perfume—
That is why the maidens love you.

Draw me!—
We will follow you eagerly!
Bring me, O King, to your chambers.

IN THIS WORLD

On this world
love has no color—
yet how deeply
my body
is stained by yours.

IZUMI SHIKIBU
[C. 974–C. 1034]

———

TO ELECTRA

I dare not ask a kiss,
  I dare not beg a smile,
Lest having that, or this,
  I might grow proud the while.

No, no, the utmost share
  Of my desire shall be
Only to kiss that air
  That lately kissed thee.

ROBERT HERRICK
[1591–1674]

The lover is forever like a drunkard
whose secrets pull out,
forever mad, frenzied, and in love.
To be self-conscious is to worry about everything,
but once drunk, what will be will be.

RUMI
[1207–1273]

PORTRAIT OF A LADY

*Y*our thighs are appletrees
whose blossoms touch the sky.
Which sky? The sky
where Watteau hung a lady's
slipper. Your knees
are a southern breeze—or
a gust of snow. Agh! what
sort of man was Fragonard?
—as if that answered
anything. Ah, yes—below
the knees, since the tune
drops that way, it is
one of those white summer days,
the tall grass of your ankles
flickers upon the shore—
Which shore?—
the sand clings to my lips—
Which shore?
Agh, petals maybe. How
should I know?
Which shore? Which shore?
I said petals from an appletree.

WILLIAM CARLOS WILLIAMS
[1883–1963]

LIFE-IN-LOVE

*N*ot in thy body is thy life at all
But in this lady's lips and hands and eyes;
Through these she yields thee life that vivifies
What else were sorrow's servant and death's thrall.
Look on thyself without her, and recall
The waste remembrance and forlorn surmise
That liv'd but in a dead-drawn breath of sighs
O'er vanish'd hours and hours eventual.

Even so much life hath the poor tress of hair
Which, stor'd apart, is all love hath to show
For heart-beats and for fire-heats long ago;
Even so much life endures unknown, even where,
'Mid change the changeless night environeth,
Lies all that golden hair undimm'd in death.

DANTE GABRIEL ROSSETTI
[1828–1882]

THE QUARREL

Suddenly, after the quarrel, while we waited,
Disheartened, silent, with downcast looks, nor stirred
Eyelid nor finger, hopeless both, yet hoping
Against all hope to unsay the sundering word:

While all the room's stillness deepened, deepened
      about us,
And each of us crept his thought's way to discover
How, with as little sound as the fall of a leaf,
The shadow had fallen, and lover quarreled with lover;

And while, in the quiet, I marveled—alas, alas—
At your deep beauty, your tragic beauty, torn
As the pale flower is torn by the wanton sparrow—
This beauty, pitied and loved, and now forsworn;

It was then, when the instant darkened to its darkest,—
When faith was lost with hope, and the rain conspired
To strike its gray arpeggios against our heartstrings,—
When love no longer dared, and scarcely desired:

It was then that suddenly, in the neighbor's room,
The music started: that brave quartette of strings
Breaking out of the stillness, as out of our stillness,
Like the indomitable heart of life that sings

When all is lost; and startled from our sorrow,
Tranced from our grief by that diviner grief,
We raised remembering eyes, each looked at other,
Blinded with tears of joy; and another leaf

Fell silently as that first; and in the instant
The shadow had gone, our quarrel became absurd;
And we rose, to the angelic voices of the music,
And I touched your hand, and we kissed, without a
          word.

CONRAD AIKEN
[1889–1973]

MY LONGING FOR YOU

My longing for you—
Too strong to keep within bounds.
At least no one can blame me
When I go to you at night
Along the road of dreams.

ONO NO KOMACHI
[C. 834–?]

KORE (EXCERPTS)

γ

*Y*ou were shaking and an air full of leaves
flowed out of the dark falls of your hair
down over the rapids of your knees
until I touched you and you grew quiet
and raised to me
your hands and your eyes and showed me
twice my face burning in amber

. . . .

τ

Morning to morning
the same door opening inward
from both sides
laugh close as you are
it is cold in the house
and I burned up all the matches in the night
to look at you

W. S. MERWIN
[1927–]

A ROSE BETWEEN THE SHEETS

Taffeta for you and taffeta for me, a rose
between the sheets and one sitting on my finger
as if it were a ruben-stein; a dress
you held once in your arms against your face
and one I lifted over your waist and spread
like a noisy pillow; you in your silk and me
in my leather jacket, nothing else, raw silk
for you, cowhide for me, and velvet
on your lips, your cheek on fire, the red of the one
against the red of the other; lustrous, I'd say;
and always bright, and always florid, and ready
always to escape; your marriage for you
and mine for me, wool, wool, in my face
and cotton in my arms, a linen once I touched
with such a silly reverence, and burlap
with the loose weave, the smell of burlap, and crepe,
the way it draped, the way it absorbed the light,
and lace for romance, and corduroy for romance,
and satin for you, and satin for me, and creases
and buttons, a kind of board, I'd say, a bed,
a cushion for your ear, maybe green, maybe
gray for your hair—and blue for me, or peach—
I love the peach—a scarf for you, a scarf
for me, a white carnation for the cold,
a sunburst, a rose of Sharon for the darkness.

GERALD STERN
[1925–]

my love

*m*y love
thy hair is one kingdom
    the king whereof is darkness
thy forehead is flight of flowers

thy head is a quick forest
    filled with sleeping birds
thy breasts are swarms of white bees
    upon the bough of thy body
thy body to me is April
in whose armpits is the approach of spring

thy thighs are white horses yoked to a chariot of kings
they are the striking of a good minstrel
between them always is a pleasant song

my love
thy head is a casket
    of the cool jewel of thy mind
the hair of thy head is one warrior
    innocent of defeat
the hair upon thy shoulders is an army
    with victory and with trumpets

thy legs are the trees of dreaming
whose fruit is the very eatage of forgetfulness

thy lips are satraps in scarlet
  in whose kiss is the combining of kings
thy wrists
are holy
  which are the keepers of the keys of thy blood
thy feet upon thy ankles are flowers in vases of silver

in thy beauty is the dilemma of flutes

  thy eyes are the betrayal
of bells comprehended through incense

E. E. CUMMINGS
[1894–1962]

LOVE'S PALACE

Of the woodland and the heath,
And the hedgerows thick with may,
And the weed-flowers underneath,
And the clambering honey-sheath,
And the mosses green and grey,

And the flecks of sun and shade
Lying light upon the grass,
And the ripple in the glade,
And the songs that float and fade,
And the joys that come and pass,

If the dog-rose choir of bees
Whirling golden in the sun,
And the sweetness of the breeze,
And the joists of mighty trees,
And the hoods of purple nun,

If this fabric of delight
Spread around to make the spring
Could but read my wish aright,
Could but aid me as it might,
Could obey me while I sing,

I should build thee such a bower
As the fairies built of old,
Walled with every fragrant flower,
And with many a mighty tower
Domed with purest morning gold.

And thy breath should draw the rose,
And thine ears be filled with sweet
Such as never poet knows,
Such as tricks him while it flows,
And eludes his bar and beat.

And thy couch should be more soft
Than the silk of Eastern days,
Than the rainbow's flush aloft,
Than the dawning clouds that oft
Melt before us as we gaze.

There my dearest love should rest
Like a bird upon the bough,
Like a fledgeling in its nest,
Like her head upon my breast,
Like my kiss upon her brow.

ARTHUR MAQUARIE
[1874–?]

THINGS SEEN

There is no natural scenery like this:
when her loose gown from her shoulders
falls, the light hardens, shadows
move slowly, my breath catches.

The flame of the blue cornflower,
a half inch above the flower,
fanned by wind.

HARVEY SHAPIRO
[1924–]

THE FIRST KISS OF LOVE (EXCERPTS)

❁

*A*way with your fictions of flimsy romance;
Those tissues of falsehood which folly has wove!
Give me the mild beam of the soul-breathing glance,
Or the rapture which dwells on the first kiss of love.

. . . .

Oh! cease to affirm that man, since his birth,
From Adam till now, has with wretchedness strove,
Some portion of paradise still is on earth,
And Eden revives in the first kiss of love.

When age chills the blood, when our pleasures are
        past—
For years fleet away with the wings of the dove—
The dearest rememberance will still be the last,
Our sweetest memorial the first kiss of love.

LORD BYRON
[1788–1824]

——

LOVE'S DRAFT

The draft of love was cool and sweet
You gave me in the cup,
But, ah, love's fire is keen and fleet,
And I am burning up.
Unless the tears I shed for you
Shall quench this burning flame,
It will consume me through and through,
And leave but ash—a name.

PAUL LAURENCE DUNBAR
[1872–1906]

A PORTRAIT

My Infelice's face, her brow, her eye,
The dimple on her cheek; and such sweet skill
Hath from the cunning workman's pencil flown,
These lips look fresh and lovely as her own.
False colours last after the true be dead.
Of all the roses grafted on her cheeks,
Of all the graces dancing in her eyes,
Of all the music set upon her tongue,
Of all that was past woman's excellence
In her white bosom; look, a painted board
Circumscribes all.

THOMAS DEKKER
[c. 1572–c. 1632]

REMEMBRANCE
For Paul

*Y*our hands easy
weight, teasing the bees
hived in my hair, your smile at the
slope of my cheek. On the
occasion, you press
above me, glowing, spouting
readiness, mystery rapes
my reason.

When you have withdrawn
your self and the magic, when
only the smell of your
love lingers between
my breasts, then, only
then, can I greedily consume
your presence.

MAYA ANGELOU
[1928–]

THE DREAM

Dear love, for nothing less than thee
Would I have broke this happy dream;
   It was a theme
For reason, much too strong for fantasy,
Therefore thou wak'd'st me wisely; yet
My dream thou brok'st not, but continued'st it.
Thou art so true that thoughts of thee suffice
To make dreams truths, and fables histories;
Enter these arms, for since thou thought'st it best,
Not to dream all my dream, let's act the rest.

As lightning, or a taper's light,
Thine eyes, and not thy noise wak'd me;
   Yet I thought thee
(For thou lovest truth) an angel, at first sight;
But when I saw thou sawest my heart,
And knew'st my thoughts, beyond an angel's art,
When thou knew'st what I dreamt, when thou knew'st
       when
Excess of joy would wake me, and cam'st then,
I must confess, it could not choose but be
Profane, to think thee any thing but thee.

Coming and staying show'd thee, thee,
But rising makes me doubt, that now
    Thou art not thou.
That love is weak where fear's as strong as he;
'Tis not all spirit, pure and brave,
If mixture it of fear, shame, honour have;
Perchance as torches, which must ready be,
Men light and put out, so thou deal'st with me;
Thou cam'st to kindle, goest to come; then I
Will dream that hope again, but else would die.

JOHN DONNE
[1572–1631]

_____

BEAT AGAINST ME NO LONGER

Ai-yee! My Yellow-Bird-Woman,
My né-ne-moosh, ai-yee! my Loved-One,
Be not afraid of my eyes!
Beat against me no longer!
Come! Come with a yielding of limbs!
Ai-yee! Woman, woman,
Trembling there in the teepee
Like the doe in the season of mating,
Why foolishly fearest thou me?
Cast the strange doubts from thy bosom!
Be not afraid of my eyes!
Be not as the flat-breasted squáw-sich
Who feels the first womanly yearnings
And hides, by the law of our people,
Alone three sleeps in the forest;
Be not as that brooding young maiden
Who wanders forlorn in the cedars,
And slumbers with troubled dreams,
To awaken suddenly, fearing
The hot throbbing blood in her bosom,
The strange eager life in her limbs.
Ai-yee! Foolish one, woman,
Cast the strange fears from thy heart!
Wash the red shame from thy face!
Be not afraid of my glances!
Be as the young silver birch
In the Moon-of-the-Green-Growing-Flowers—
Who sings with the thrill of the sap

As it leaps to the south wind's caresses;
Who yields her rain-swollen buds
To the kiss of the sun with glad dancing.
Be as the cool tranquil moon
Who flings off her silver-blue blanket
To bare her white breast to the pine;
Who walks through the many-eyed night
In her gleaming white nudeness
With proud eyes that will not look down.
Be as the sun in her glory,
Who dances across the blue day,
And flings her red soul, fierce-burning,
Into the arms of the twilight.
Ai-yee! Foolish one, woman,
Be as the sun and the moon!
Cast the strange doubts from thy bosom!
Wash the red shame from thy face!
Thou art a woman, a woman!
Beat against me no longer!
Be not afraid of my eyes!

LEW SARETT
[1888–1954]

MOSCOW
For Diane Freund

I love to bend down over my love,
my crayon at her breast, my lips just over her neck.
I love her eyes following my left hand,
her fingers rubbing the Greek blanket.
I love the sunlight on the cold windows,
the horns of Scriabin rising through the dreary street,
the carved houses forever on our wild faces.

GERALD STERN
[1925–]

LIFE IN A LOVE

Escape me?
Never—
Beloved!
While I am I, and you are you,
    So long as the world contains us both,
    Me the loving and you the loth,
While the one eludes, must the other pursue.
My life is a fault at last, I fear:
It seems too much like a fate, indeed!
Though I do my best I shall scarce succeed.
But what if I fail of my purpose here?
It is but to keep the nerves at strain,
To dry one's eyes and laugh at a fall,
And, baffled, get up and begin again,—
So the chace takes up one's life, that's all.
While, look but once from your farthest bound
At me so deep in the dust and dark,
No sooner the old hope goes to ground
Than a new one, straight to the self-same mark,
I shape me—
Ever
Removed!

ROBERT BROWNING
[1812–1889]

DELIA (VI)

Fair is my love, and cruel as she's fair:
Her brow shades frowns although her eyes are sunny,
Her smiles are lightning though her pride despair,
And her disdains are gall, her favours honey;
A modest maid, deck'd with a blush of honour,
Whose feet do tread green paths of youth and love,
The wonder of all eyes that look upon her:
Sacred on earth, design'd a saint above.
Chastity and beauty, which were deadly foes,
Live reconciled friends within her brow;
And had she pity to conjoin with those,
Then who had heard the plaints I utter now?
For had she not been fair and thus unkind,
My muse had slept, and none had known my mind.

SAMUEL DANIEL
[1562–1619]

PRIVATE WORSHIP

*S*he lay there in the stone folds of his life
Like a blue flower in granite—this he knew;
And knew how now inextricably the petals
Clung to the rock; recessed beyond his hand-thrust;
More deeply in, past more forgotten windings
Than his rude tongue could utter, praising her.

He praised her with his eyes, beholding oddly
Not what another saw, but what she added—
Thinning today and shattering with a slow smile—
To the small flower within, to the saved secret.
She was not to have—except that something,
Always like petals falling, entered him.

She was not his to keep—except the brightness,
Flowing from her, that lived in him like dew;
And the kind flesh he could remember touching,
And the unconscious lips, and both her eyes:
These lay in him like leaves—beyond the last turn
Breathing the rocky darkness till it bloomed.

It was not large, this chamber of the blue flower,
Nor could the scent escape; nor the least color
Ebb from that place and stain the outer stone.
Nothing upon his grey sides told the fable,
Nothing of love or lightness, nothing of song;
Nothing of her at all. Yet he could fancy—

———

Oh, he could feel where petals spread their softness,
Gathered from windfalls of her when she smiled;
Growing some days, he thought, as if to burst him—
Oh, he could see the split halves, and the torn flower
Fluttering in sudden sun; and see the great stain—
Oh, he could see what tears had done to stone.

MARK VAN DOREN
[1894–1972]

i like my body when it is with your

i like my body when it is with your
body. It is so quite new a thing.
Muscles better and nerves more.
i like your body. i like what it does,
i like its hows. i like to feel the spine
of your body and its bones, and the trembling
-firm-smooth ness and which i will
again and again and again
kiss, i like kissing this and that of you,
i like, slowly stroking the, shocking fuzz
of your electric furr, and what-is-it comes
over parting flesh. . . . And eyes big love-crumbs,

and possibly i like the thrill

of under me you so quite new

E. E. CUMMINGS
[1894–1962]

81

LA FIGLIA CHE PIANGE

Stand on the highest pavement of the stair—
Lean on a garden urn—
Weave, weave the sunlight in your hair—
Clasp your flowers to you with a pained surprise—
Fling them to the ground and turn
With a fugitive resentment in your eyes:
But weave, weave the sunlight in your hair.

So I would have had him leave,
So I would have had her stand and grieve,
So he would have left
As the soul leaves the body torn and bruised,
As the mind deserts the body it has used.
I should find
Some way incomparably light and deft,
Some way we both should understand,
Simple and faithless as a smile and shake of the hand.
She turned away, but with the autumn weather
Compelled my imagination many days,
Many days and many hours:
Her hair over her arms and her arms full of flowers.
And I wonder how they should have been together!
I should have lost a gesture and a pose.
Sometimes these cogitations still amaze
The troubled midnight and the noon's repose.

T. S. Eliot
[1888–1965]

82

LEDA

*W*here the slow river
meets the tide,
a red swan lifts red wings
and darker beak,
and underneath the purple down
of his soft breast
uncurls his coral feet.

Through the deep purple
of the dying heat
of sun and mist,
the level ray of sun-beam
has caressed
the lily with dark breast,
and flecked with richer gold
its golden crest.

Where the slow lifting
of the tide,
floats into the river
and slowly drifts
among the reeds,
and lifts the yellow flags,
he floats
where tide and river meet.

Ah kingly kiss—
no more regret
nor old deep memories
to mar the bliss;
where the low sedge is thick,
the gold day-lily
outspreads and rests
beneath soft fluttering
of red swan wings
and the warm quivering
of the red swan's breast.

HILDA DOOLITTLE
[1886–1961]

TO ALTHEA, FROM PRISON

*W*hen Love with unconfined wings
Hovers within my gates,
And my divine Althea brings
To whisper at the grates;
When I lie tangled in her hair,
And fetter'd to her eye,
The gods, that wanton in the air,
Know no such liberty.

When flowing cups run swiftly round
With no allaying Thames,
Our careless heads with roses bound,
Our hearts with loyal flames;
When thirsty grief in wine we steep,
When healths and draughts go free,
Fishes, that tipple in the deep,
Know no such liberty.

When (like committed linnets) I
With shriller throat shall sing
The sweetness, mercy, majesty,
And glories of my king;
When I shall voice aloud how good
He is, how great should be,
Enlarged winds, that curl the flood,
Know no such liberty.

Stone walls do not a prison make,
Nor iron bars a cage;
Minds innocent and quiet take
That for an hermitage;
If I have freedom in my love,
And in my soul am free,
Angels alone that soar above,
Enjoy such liberty.

RICHARD LOVELACE
[1618–1657]

———

SONG OF LOVE

*H*ow shall I guard my soul so that it be
Touched not by thine?
And how shall it be brought,
Lifted above thee unto other things?
Ah, gladly would I hide it utterly
Lost in the dark
Where there are no murmurings
In strange and silent
Places that do not
Vibrate when thy deep soul quivers and sings.
But all that touches us two makes us twin,
Even as the bow crossing the violin,
Draws but one voice from the two strings that meet.
Upon what instrument are we two spanned?
And what great player has us in his hand?
O song most sweet.

RAINER MARIA RILKE
[1875–1926]

HIS SONG OF THE GREEN WILLOW

I guide my darling under the willow tree
to increase the flow of her blood.

A branch weeps, so does she, a twig breaks off
like one of her thoughts.

We are helpless together, we spend the night
listening to shameless sounds

and study the moon together, watching it spread
knowledge over the white mulberry.

Whoever lies down first, that one will hear
the cardinal first, and that one will see the streaks

above the lilacs. Whoever does not leave,
whoever is loyal, whoever stays, that one will see

the rabbits thinking, that one will see a nest
and small ones warm from living. Whoever sits up

and looks at the sky—whoever is alone—
that one will be the griever, that one will make

his song out of nothing, that one will lean on his side
and stir the ground with his stick—and break his
        stick—

if that is his way, and moan, if that is his way,
and go on forever—his thirty-two feet at a time—

thirty-two feet until the branches start
and the scattered twigs,

her thoughts again—for him her thoughts—his song
of the green willow, her song of pain and severance.

GERALD STERN
[1925–]

TO HIS MISTRESS

*W*hy dost thou shade thy lovely face? O why
Does that eclipsing hand of thine deny
The sunshine of the Sun's enlivening eye?

Without thy light what light remains in me?
Thou art my life; my way, my light's in thee;
I live, I move, and by thy beams I see.

Thou art my life—if thou but turn away
My life's a thousand deaths. Thou art my way—
Without thee, Love, I travel not but stray.

My light thou art—without thy glorious sight
My eyes are darken'd with eternal night.
My Love, thou art my way, my life, my light.

Thou art my way; I wander if thou fly.
Thou art my light; if hid, how blind am I!
Thou art my life; if thou withdraw'st, I die.

My eyes are dark and blind; I cannot see:
To whom or whither should my darkness flee,
But to that light?—and who's that light but thee?

If I have lost my path, dear lover, say,
Shall I still wander in a doubtful way?
Love, shall a lamb of Israel's sheepfold stray?

———

My path is lost, my wandering steps do stray;
I cannot go, nor can I safely stay;
Whom should I seek but thee, my path, my way?

And yet thou turn'st thy face away and fly'st me!
And yet I sue for grace and thou deny'st me!
Speak, art thou angry, Love, or only try'st me?

Thou art the pilgrim's path, the blind man's eye,
The dead man's life. On thee my hopes rely:
If I but them remove, I surely die.

Dissolve thy sunbeams, close thy wings and stay!
See, see how I am blind, and dead, and stray!
—O thou art my life, my light, my way!

Then work thy will! If passion bid me flee,
My reason shall obey, my wings shall be
Stretch'd out no farther than from me to thee!

JOHN WILMOT, EARL OF ROCHESTER
[1647–1680]

LOVE'S UNION
SONG OF SONGS 1:12–15

For the king's banquet
My nard gives forth its fragrance.
My love is for me a sachet of myrrh
To rest in my bosom.
My lover is for me a cluster of henna
From the vineyards of Engedi.

Ah, you are beautiful my beloved,
Ah, you are beautiful; your eyes are doves

I SING THE BODY ELECTRIC (EXCERPT)

This is the female form,
A divine nimbus exhales from it from head to foot,
It attracts with fierce undeniable attraction,
I am drawn by its breath as if I were no more than a
    helpless vapour, all falls aside but myself and it,
Books, art, religion, time, and the visible and solid
            earth,
    and what was expected of heaven or feared of hell,
    are now consumed,
Mad filaments, ungovernable shoots play out of it, the
    response likewise ungovernable,
Ebb stung by the flow and flow stung by the ebb, love-
    flesh swelling and deliciously aching,
Limitless limpid jets of love hot and enormous,
    quivering jelly of love, white-blow and delirious
    juice,
Bridegroom might of love working surely and softly
    into the prostrate dawn,
Undulating into the willing and yielding day,
Lost in the cleave of the clasping and sweet-fleshed
    day.

This the nucleus—after the child is born of woman,
    man is born of woman,
This the bath of birth, this the merge of small and
    large, and the outlet again.
Be not ashamed women, your privilege encloses the
    rest, and is the exit of the rest,

You are the gates of the body, and you are the gates of
the soul.
The female contains all qualities and tempers then,
She is in her place and moves with perfect balance,
She is all things duly veiled, she is both passive and
active,
She is to conceive daughters as well as sons, and sons
as well as daughters.

As I see my soul reflected in Nature,
As I see through a mist, One with inexpressible
completeness, sanity, beauty,
See the bent head and arms folded over the breast, the
Female I see.

WALT WHITMAN
[1819–1892]

———

III

Reflections of Love

IN MUTUAL EMBRACE

The desire in the female for the male
is so that they may perfect each other's work.
God put desire in man and woman
in order that the world
should be preserved by this union.
God instills the desire of every part for the other:
from their union, creation results.
And so night and day are in mutual embrace:
they appear to be opposites, even enemies,
but the truth they serve is one,
each desiring the other like kin,
for the perfection of their work.
Both serve one purpose, for without night,
human nature would receive no income:
what then could day expend?

RUMI
[1207–1273]

HER BEAUTIFUL HANDS

O your hands—they are strangely fair!
Fair—for the jewels that sparkle there,—
Fair—for the witchery of the spell
That ivory keys alone can tell;
But when their delicate touches rest
Here in my own do I love them best,
As I clasp with eager, acquisitive spans
My glorious treasure of beautiful hands!

Marvelous—wonderful—beautiful hands!
They can coax roses to bloom in the strands
Of your brown tresses; and ribbons will twine,
Under mysterious touches of thine,
Into such knots as entangle the soul
And fetter the heart under such a control
As only the strength of my love understands—
My passionate love for your beautiful hands.

As I remember the first fair touch
Of those beautiful hands that I love so much,
I seem to thrill as I then was thrilled,
Kissing the glove that I found unfilled—
When I met your gaze, and the queenly bow,
As you said to me, laughingly, "Keep it now!". . .
And dazed and alone in a dream I stand,
Kissing this ghost of your beautiful hand.

When first I loved, in the long ago,
And held your hand as I told you so—
Pressed and caressed it and gave it a kiss
And said "I could die for a hand like this!"
Little I dreamed love's fullness yet
Had to ripen when eyes were wet
And prayers were vain in their wild demands
For one warm touch of your beautiful hands.

Beautiful Hands!—O Beautiful Hands!
Could you reach out of the alien lands
Where you are lingering, and give me, to-night
Only a touch—were it ever so light—
My heart were soothed, and my weary brain
Would lull itself into rest again;
For there is no solace the world commands
Like the caress of your beautiful hands.

JAMES WHITCOMB RILEY
[1849–1916]

THAT TIME OF YEAR
THOU MAYST IN ME BEHOLD

That time of year thou mayst in me behold
When yellow leaves, or none, or few, do hang
Upon those boughs which shake against the cold,
Bare ruined choirs where late the sweet birds sang.
In me thou seest the twilight of such day
As after sunset fadeth in the west,
Which by and by black night doth take away,
Death's second self, that seals up all in rest.
In me thou seest the glowing of such fire
That on the ashes of his youth doth lie,
As the deathbed whereon it must expire,
Consumed with that which it was nourished by.
    This thou perceiv'st, which makes thy love more
        strong,
    To love that well which thou must leave ere long.

WILLIAM SHAKESPEARE
[1564–1616]

HER FACE

Her face
so fair
first bent
mine eye

Her tongue
so sweet
then drew
mine ear

Her wit
so sharp
then hit
my heart

Mine eye
to like
her face
doth lead

Mine ear
to learn
her tongue
doth teach

My heart
to love
her wit
doth move

Her face
with beams
doth blind
mine eye

Her tongue
with sound
doth charm
mine ear

Her wit
with art
doth knit
my heart

Mine eye
with life
her face
doth feed

Mine ear
with hope
her tongue
doth feast

My heart
with skill
her wit
doth fill

O face
with frowns
wrong not
mine eye

O tongue
with cheeks
vex not
mine ear

O wit
with smart
wound not
my heart

This eye   This ear   This heart
shall joy   shall yield   shall swear
her face   her tongue   her wit
to serve   to trust   to fear.

SIR ARTHUR GORGES
[1557–1625]

A DREAM

*D*ear, though the night is gone,
Its dream still haunts today,
That brought us to a room
Cavernous, lofty as
A railway terminus,
And crowded in that gloom
Were beds, and we in one
In a far corner lay.

Our whisper woke no clocks,
We kissed and I was glad
At everything you did,
Indifferent to those
Who sat with hostile eyes
In pairs on every bed,
Arms round each other's neck,
Inert and vaguely sad.

What buried worm of guilt
Or what malignant doubt
Am I the victim of,
That you then, unabashed,
Did what I never wished,
Confessed another love;
And I, submissive, felt
Unwanted and went out?

W. H. AUDEN
[1907–1973]

AT THE MID HOUR OF NIGHT

❀

At the mid hour of night, when stars are weeping,
    I fly
To the lone vale we loved, when life shone warm in
        thine eye;
And I think oft, if spirits can steal from the regions of
        air
To revisit past scenes of delight, thou wilt come to me
        there.
And tell me our love is remember'd even in the sky.

Then I sing the wild song it once was rapture to hear,
When our voices commingling breathed like one on
        the ear;
And as Echo far off through the vale my sad orison
        rolls,
I think, O my love! 'tis thy voice from the Kingdom of
        souls
Faintly answering still the notes that once were so
        dear.

THOMAS MOORE
[1779–1852]

————

104

I USED UP THIS BODY

I used up this body
longing
for one who does not come.
A deep valley, now,
what once was my heart.

IZUMI SHIKIBU
[C. 974–C. 1034]

LOVE, THE WIZARD

$\mathcal{L}$ove stole in to a fair child dreaming
'Mid birds and butterflies—
He kissed her innocent eyes.
He held his cruse o'er her bright head gleaming;
The wine and oil to her feet went streaming;
And the child was a woman wise.

Love crept in to a woman gazing,
Who saw, with eyes of pain,
A garden wet with rain.
Her faded face with his right hand raising,
He wrapped her in rainbow vesture blazing;
And the woman was young again.

LILIAN WOOSTER GREAVES
(DATES UNKNOWN)

SO WHAT IS LOVE?

So what is love? If thou wouldst know
The human heart alone can tell:
Two minds with but a single thought,
Two hearts that beat as one.

And whence comes Love? Like morning bright
Love comes without thy call.
And how dies Love? A spirit bright,
Love never dies at all.

MARIA LOVELL
[1803–1877]

LINES

When the beautiful star of the West moves on,
A lonely gem, through the fields of air;
When the last faint flush of the sun-light's gone
And no beams but her own are shining there;
Steal through the shades of the twilight love!
The spell of that gentlest hour to prove.

It sinks on the spirit like some sweet balm,
Shed o'er us from brighter, and happier spheres;
And in suffering bosoms its touching calm
Awakens the source of delicious tears;
While dark and passionate thoughts, to rest
Are hush'd in the haughty, and erring breast.

ELIZA ACTON
[1799–1859]

ADAM AND EVE

*W*hen the first dark had fallen around them
And the leaves were weary of praise,
In the clear silence Beauty found them
And shewed them all her ways.

In the high noon of the heavenly garden
Where the angels sunned with the birds,
Beauty, before their hearts could harden,
Had taught them heavenly words.

When they fled in the burning weather
And nothing dawned but a dream,
Beauty fasted their hands together
And cooled them at her stream.

And when day wearied and night grew stronger,
And they slept as the beautiful must,
Then she bided a little longer,
And blossomed from their dust.

MARJORIE PICKTHALL
[1883–1922]

CUPID AND MY CAMPASPE PLAY'D

Cupid and my Campaspe play'd
At cards for kisses—Cupid paid:
He stakes his quiver, bow and arrows,
His mother's doves, and team of sparrows;
Loses them too; then down he throws
The coral of his lip, the rose
Growing on 's cheek (but none knows how);
With these, the crystal of his brow,
And then the dimple of his chin:
All these did my Campaspe win.
At last he set her both his eyes,
She won, and Cupid blind did rise.
O Love! has she done this to thee?
What shall (alas!) become of me?

JOHN LYLY
[c. 1554–1606]

THE FLEA

Mark but this flea, and mark in this,
How little that which thou deny'st me is;
Me it sucked first, and now sucks thee,
And in this flea, our two bloods mingled be;
Confess it, this cannot be said
A sin, or shame, or loss of maidenhead,
   Yet this enjoys before it woo,
    And pampered swells with one blood made of two,
    And this, alas, is more than we would do.

Oh stay, three lives in one flea spare,
Where we almost, nay more than married are.
This flea is you and I, and this
Our marriage bed, and marriage temple is;
Though parents grudge, and you, we'are met,
And cloistered in these living walls of jet.
   Though use make you apt to kill me,
    Let not to this, self murder added be,
    And sacrilege, three sins in killing three.

Cruel and sudden, hast thou since
Purpled thy nail, in blood of innocence?
In what could this flea guilty be,
Except in that drop which it sucked from thee?
Yet thou triumph'st, and say'st that thou
Find'st not thyself, nor me the weaker now;
    'Tis true, then learn how false, fears be;
    Just so much honour, when thou yield'st to me,
    Will waste, as this flea's death took life from thee.

JOHN DONNE
[1572–1631]

WITH A FLOWER

I hide myself within a flower
That wearing on your breast,
You, unsuspecting, wear me too—
And angels know the rest.

I hide myself within my flower,
That, fading from your vase,
You, unsuspecting, feel for me
Almost a loneliness.

EMILY DICKINSON
[1830–1886]

———

LOVE'S COMING

Quietly as rosebuds
Talk to thin air,
Love came so lightly
I knew not he was there.

Quietly as lovers
Creep at the middle noon,
Softly as players tremble
In the tears of a tune;

Quietly as lilies
Their faint vows declare,
Came the shy pilgrim:
I knew not he was there.

Quietly as tears fall
On a warm sin,
Softly as griefs call
In a violin;

Without hail or tempest,
Blue sword or flame,
Love came so lightly
I knew not that he came.

SHAW NEILSON
[1872–1942]

LOVE'S LANGUAGE (EXCERPT)

How does Love speak?
In the proud spirit suddenly grown meek—
The haughty heart grown humble; in the tender
And unnamed light that floods the world with
        splendor;
In the resemblance which the fond eyes trace
In all fair things to one beloved face;
In the shy touch of hands that thrill and tremble—
In looks and lips that can no more dissemble—
Thus doth Love speak?

How does Love speak?
In the wild words that uttered seem so weak
They shrink ashamed to silence; in the fire
Glance strikes with glance, swift flashing high and
        higher,
Like lightnings that precede the mighty storm;
In the deep, soulful stillness; in the warm,
Impassioned tide that sweeps through throbbing veins,
Between the shores of keen delight and pains;
In the embrace where madness melts in bliss,
And in the convulsive rapture of a kiss—
Thus doth Love speak.

ELLA WHEELER WILCOX
[1850–1919]

LOVE LIVES BEYOND

*L*ove lives beyond
The tomb, the earth, which fades like dew!
I love the fond,
The faithful, and the true.

Love lives in sleep,
The happiness of healthy dreams;
Eve's dews may weep,
But love delightful seems.

'Tis seen in flowers,
And in the morning's pearly dew;
In earth's green hours,
And in the heaven's eternal blue.

'Tis heard in spring
When light and sunbeams, warm and kind,
On angel's wing
Bring love and music to the mind.

And where is voice,
So young, so beautiful, and sweet
As nature's choice,
Where spring and lovers meet?

Love lives beyond
The tomb, the earth, the flowers, and dew.
I love the fond,
The faithful, young, and true.

JOHN CLARE
[1793–1864]

NEW MOON

❀

I am in love
with a man
who is gone now
hunting
for vision
His bones
know the
scent of it
His hands full of
intuition
and praise
What he lacks
he seeks
And I watch him
from my hill
As he treads
the countryside
and splits the great
and fertile valleys
like the hips of
a woman
he has loved
for centuries
in many forms
   As an eagle
   a warrior
   a stone

I love him

Over there

Far from me

JEWEL KILCHER
[1974–]

PASSION UNINSPIRED BY SENTIMENT

Addressed to him who denied their existing together.

Oh! Passion, seducer of heart and of soul!
Thou transport tyrannic! half pleasure, half pain!
Why consum'st thou the breast with such madd'ning
       controul?
Fly quickly—yet, ah! come as quickly again.

Without thee, what's life but a wilderness drear,
Or a chill, gloomy vale, where stern apathy reigns?
Like Phoebus, thy vivid refulgence can cheer,
And brighten, in rapture, e'en Memory's pains.

When pleasure seduces the wild throbbing heart
In moments ecstatic of tender excess,
When Fancy refines, and when Passion takes part,
The lover existence too fondly may bless.

Yet Passion alone, to the delicate mind,
Aspires not a simple sensation above;
Unless sentiment yield it an ardour refin'd,
It degrades, not ennobles the essence of love.

CHARLOTTE DACRE
[1782–C. 1841]

SAPPHO AND PHAO (EXCERPT)

VI

Is it to love, to fix the tender gaze,
To hide the timid blush, and steal away;
To shun the busy world, and waste the day
In some rude mountain's solitary maze?
Is it to chant one name in ceaseless lays,
To hear no words that other tongues can say,
To watch the pale moon's melancholy ray,
To chide in fondness, and in folly praise?
Is it to pour th' involuntary sigh,
To dream of bliss, and wake new pangs to prove;
To talk, in fancy, with the speaking eye,
Then start with jealousy, and wildly rove;
Is it to loathe the light, and wish to die?
For these I feel,—and feel that they are Love.

XVII

Love steals unheeded o'er the tranquil mind,
As Summer breezes fan the sleeping main,
Slow through each fibre creeps the subtle pain,
'Till closely round the yielding bosom twin'd.
Vain is the hope the magic to unbind,
The potent mischief riots in the brain,
Grasps ev'ry thought, and burns in ev'ry vein,

'Till in the heart the Tyrant lives enshrin'd.
Oh! Victor strong! bending the vanquish'd frame;
Sweet is the thraldom that thou bid'st us prove!
And sacred is the tear thy victims claim,
For blest are those whom sighs of sorrow move!
Then nymphs beware how ye profane my name,
Nor blame my weakness, till like me ye love!

MARY ROBINSON
[1758–1800]

OVERLOOKED

Sleep, with her tender balm, her touch so kind,
   has passed me by:
Afar I see her vesture, velvet-lined,
   float silently;
O! Sleep, my tired eyes had need of thee!
Is thy sweet kiss not meant to-night for me?

Peace, with the blessings that I longed for so,
   has passed me by;
Where'er she folds her holy wings I know
   all tempests die;
O! Peace, my tired soul had need of thee!
Is thy sweet kiss denied alone to me?

Love, with her heated touches, passion-stirred,
   has passed me by.
I called, "O stay thy flight," but all unheard
   my lonely cry:
O! Love, my tired heart had need of thee!
Is thy sweet kiss withheld alone from me?

Sleep, sister-twin of Peace, my waking eyes
   so weary grow!
O! Love, thou wanderer from Paradise,
   dost thou not know
How oft my lonely heart has cried to thee?
But Thou, and Sleep, and Peace, come not to me.

EMILY PAULINE JOHNSON
(AKA TEKAHIONWAKE)
[1861–1913]

LOVE-LILY

*B*etween the hands, between the brows,
Between the lips of Love-Lily,
A spirit is born whose birth endows
My blood with fire to burn through me;
Who breathes upon my gazing eyes,
Who laughs and murmurs in mine ear,
At whose least touch my colour flies,
And whom my life grows faint to hear.

Within the voice, within the heart,
Within the mind of Love-Lily,
A spirit is born who lifts apart
His tremulous wings and looks at me;
Who on my mouth his finger lays,
And shows, while whispering lutes confer,
That Eden of Love's watered ways
Whose winds and spirits worship her.

Brows, hands, and lips, heart, mind, and voice,
Kisses and words of Love-Lily,—
Oh! bid me with your joy rejoice
Till riotous longing rest in me!
Ah! let not hope be still distraught,
But find in her its gracious goal,
Whose speech Truth knows not from her thought
Nor Love her body from her soul.

DANTE GABRIEL ROSSETTI
[1828–1882]

125

EBB

I know what my heart is like
   Since your love died:
It is like a hollow ledge
Holding a little pool
   Left there by the tide,
     A little tepid pool,
Drying inward from the edge.

EDNA ST. VINCENT MILLAY
[1892–1950]

YOU AND I

My hand is lonely for your clasping, dear;
My ear is tired waiting for your call.
I want your strength to help, your laugh to cheer;
Heart, soul and senses need you, one and all.
I droop without your full, frank sympathy;
We ought to be together—you and I;
We want each other so, to comprehend
The dream, the hope, things planned, or seen, or
       wrought.
Companion, comforter and guide and friend,
As much as love asks love, does thought ask thought.
Life is so short, so fast the lone hours fly,
We ought to be together, you and I.

HENRY ALFORD
[1810–1871]

STANZAS TO JESSY

There is a mystic thread of life
So dearly wreath'd with mine alone,
That Destiny's relentless knife
At once must sever both, or none.

There is a Form on which these eyes
Have fondly gazed with such delight—
By day, that Form their joy supplies,
And Dreams restore it, through the night.

There is a Voice whose tones inspire
Such softened feelings in my breast,
I would not hear a Seraph Choir,
Unless that voice could join the rest.

There is a Face whose Blushes tell
Affection's tale upon the cheek,
But pallid at our fond farewell,
Proclaims more love than words can speak.

There is a Lip, which mine has prest,
But none had ever prest before;
It vowed to make me sweetly blest,
That mine alone should press it more.

There is a Bosom all my own,
Has pillow'd oft this aching head,
A Mouth which smiles on me alone,
An Eye, whose tears with mine are shed.

There are two Hearts whose movements thrill,
In unison so closely sweet,
That Pulse to Pulse responsive still
They Both must heave, or cease to beat.

There are two Souls, whose equal flow
In gentle stream so calmly run,
That when they part—they part?—ah no!
They cannot part—those Souls are One.

LORD BYRON
[1788–1824]

ONE WAY OF LOVE

I

All June I bound the rose in sheaves.
Now, rose by rose, I strip the leaves
And strew them where Pauline may pass.
She will not turn aside? Alas!
Let them lie. Suppose they die?
The chance was they might take her eye.

II

How many a month I strove to suit
These stubborn fingers to the lute!
To-day I venture all I know.
She will not hear my music? So!
Break the string; fold music's wing:
Suppose Pauline had bade me sing!

III

My whole life long I learned to love.
This hour my utmost art I prove
And speak my passion—heaven or hell?
She will not give me heaven? 'Tis well!
Lose who may—I still can say,
Those who win heaven, blest are they!

ROBERT BROWNING
[1812–1889]

———

THE MATHEMATICIAN IN LOVE

I

$\mathcal{A}$ mathematician fell madly in love
With a lady, young, handsome, and charming:
By angles and ratios harmonic he strove
Her curves and proportions all faultless to prove.
As he scrawled hieroglyphics alarming.

II

He measured with care, from the ends of a base,
The arcs which her features subtended:
Then he framed transcendental equations, to trace
The flowing outlines of her figure and face,
And thought the result very splendid.

III

He studied (since music has charms for the fair)
The theory of fiddles and whistles,—
Then composed, by acoustic equations, an air,
Which, when 'twas performed, made the lady's long
hair
Stand on end, like a porcupine's bristles.

IV

The lady loved dancing: —he therefore applied,
To the polka and waltz, an equation;
But when to rotate on his axis he tried,
His centre of gravity swayed to one side,
And he fell, by the earth's gravitation.

V

No doubts of the fate of his suit made him pause,
For he proved, to his own satisfaction,
That the fair one returned his affection;—"because,
"As every one knows, by mechanical laws,
"Re-action is equal to action."

VI

"Let x denote beauty,—y, manners well-bred,—
"z, Fortune,—(this last is essential),—
"Let L stand for love"—our philosopher said,—
"Then L is a function of x, y, and z,
"Of the kind which is known as potential."

"Now integrate *L* with respect to *d t*,
"(*t* Standing for time and persuasion);
"Then, between proper limits, 'tis easy to see,
"The definite integral *Marriage* must be: —
"(A very concise demonstration)."

Said he—"If the wandering course of the moon
"By Algebra can be predicted,
"The female affections must yield to it soon"—
—But the lady ran off with a dashing dragoon,
And left him amazed and afflicted.

WILLIAM J. MACQUORN RANKINE
[1820–1872]

SONNETS FROM THE PORTUGUESE
(7)

The face of all the world is changed, I think,
Since first I heard the footsteps of thy soul
Move still, oh, still, beside me, as they stole
Betwixt me and the dreadful outer brink
Of obvious death, where I, who thought to sink,
Was caught up into love, and taught the whole
Of life in a new rhythm. The cup of dole
God gave for baptism, I am fain to drink,
And praise its sweetness, Sweet, with thee anear.
The names of country, heaven, are changed away
For where thou art or shalt be, there or here;
And this . . . this lute and song . . . loved yesterday,
(The singing angels know) are only dear,
Because thy name moves right in what they say.

ELIZABETH BARRETT BROWNING
[1806–1861]

CLOSE BY

So near at hand (our eyes o'erlooked its nearness
In search of distant things)
A dear dream lay—perchance to grow in dearness
Had we but felt its wings
Astir. The air our very breathing fanned
It was so near at hand.

Once, many days ago, we almost held it,
The love we so desired;
But our shut eyes saw not, and fate dispelled it
Before our pulses fired
To flame, and errant fortune bade us stand
Hand almost touching hand.

I sometimes think had we two been discerning,
The by-path hid away
From others' eyes had then revealed its turning
To us, nor led astray
Our footsteps, guiding us into love's land
That lay so near at hand.

So near at hand, dear heart, could we have known it!
Throughout those dreamy hours,
Had either loved, or loving had we shown it,
Response had sure been ours;
We did not know that heart could heart command,
And love so near at hand!

What then availed the red wine's subtle glisten?
We passed it blindly by,
And now what profit that we wait and listen
Each for the other's heart beat? Ah! the cry
Of love o'erlooked still lingers, you and I
Sought heaven afar, we did not understand
'Twas—once so near at hand.

EMILY PAULINE JOHNSON
(AKA TEKAHIONWAKE)
[1861–1913]

NO WAY TO SEE HIM

No way to see him
on this moonless night—
I lie awake longing, burning,
breasts racing fire,
heart in flames.

ONO NO KOMACHI
[c. 834–?]

LOVE SONG

Once in the world's first prime,
When nothing lived or stirred;
Nothing but new-born Time,
Nor was there even a bird—
The Silence spoke to a Star;
But I do not dare repeat
What it said to its love afar,
It was too sweet, too sweet.

But there, in the fair world's youth,
Ere sorrow had drawn breath
When nothing was known but Truth
Nor was there even death,
The Star to Silence was wed,
And the Sun was priest that day,
And they made their bridal-bed
High in the Milky Way.

For the great white star had heard
Her silent lover's speech;
It needed no passionate word
To pledge them each to each.
O lady fair and far
Hear, oh, hear, and apply!
Thou the beautiful Star—
The voiceless Silence, I.

ELLA WHEELER WILCOX
[1850–1919]

139

DAY DAWN

All yesterday the thought of you was resting in my
    soul,
And when sleep wandered o'er the world that very
    thought she stole
To fill my dreams with splendour such as stars could
    not eclipse,
And in the morn I wakened with your name upon my
    lips.

Awakened, my beloved, to the morning of your eyes,
Your splendid eyes, so full of clouds, wherein a shadow
    tries
To overcome the flame that melts into the world of
    grey,
As coming suns dissolve the dark that veils the edge of
    day.

Cool drifts the air at dawn of day, cool lies the sleeping
    dew,
But all my heart is burning, for it woke from dreams of
    you;
And O! these longing eyes of mine look out and only
    see
A dying night, a waking day, and calm on all but me.

So gently creeps the morning through the heavy air,
The dawn grey-garbed and velvet-shod is wandering
	everywhere
To wake the slumber-laden hours that leave their
	dreamless rest,
With outspread, laggard wings to court the pillows of
	the west.

Up from the earth a moisture steals with odours fresh
	and soft,
A smell of moss and grasses warm with dew, and far
	aloft
The stars are growing colourless, while drooping in the
	west,
A late, wan moon is paling in a sky of amethyst.

The passing of the shadows, as they waft their pinions
	near,
Has stirred a tender wind within the night-hushed
	atmosphere,
That in its homeless wanderings sobs in an undertone
An echo to my heart that sobbing calls for you alone.

The night is gone, beloved, and another day set free,
Another day of hunger for the one I may not see.
What care I for the perfect dawn? the blue and empty
        skies?
The night is always mine without the morning of your
        eyes.

EMILY PAULINE JOHNSON
(AKA TEKAHIONWAKE)
[1861–1913]

BEAUTY.

Spirit of Beauty! say, where is thy dwelling?
Art thou an habitant of earth or sea,—
By the bright waters of the fountain's welling,
Or in the forest liv'st thou solemnly;
And what art thou? Thou tint'st the rose, and breathest
Thy soul of sweetness 'midst its crimson folds;
And in its drooping curves the ivy wreathest,
And cast'st the violets in their fairy moulds.

Spirit of Beauty, thou dost touch the mountains,
And they are shadowed on the pale blue sky
Distant and dim, or look like silver fountains
Of light, when snows are there, and stars are high.
And the rich sunset clouds, at day's declining,
Grow glorious as bright dreams beneath thy power;
And thou art surely in the pale moon's shining,
In the lone grandeur of the midnight hour.

Spirit of Beauty, on the maiden's forehead,
Beneath her braided hair, thy spell hath been;
And in the placid eyes that once have sorrowed,
But now in holy patience shine serene;
And in the autumn groves our steps thou meetest,
Upon the fading flowers thy glories be,
The saddest music often is the sweetest,
And earth's most mournful things are full of thee.

Therefore, when fadeth some sweet lip, and paleth
The cheek, and the bright eye grows sunk and dull
Where'er the spirit o'er the clay prevaileth,
We say, we scarce know why, "How beautiful!"
And when some heart of gentle mould is broken,
Yet to the very last doth faithful prove,
Cold, cold must be the lip that hath not spoken
Of the pure beauty of a woman's love.

Spirit of Beauty! now I know thy dwelling—
'T is not in the cold earth, or sea, or air;
The human heart is thy abode, and, swelling
Its throbbing pulses, thou art shrined there.
From thence thou shinest out, and fling'st thy
        lightening,
Making even beautiful this world of strife;
Touchest the poets' songs, and fling'st thy brightening
And circling glory o'er the paths of life.

MARY ANN BROWNE GRAY
[1812–1844]

SEASONS

Sweet in summer, cups of snow,
Cooling thirsty lips aglow;
Sweet to sailors winter-bound,
Spring arrives with garlands crowned;
Sweeter yet the hour that covers
With one cloak a pair of lovers,
Living lost in golden weather,
While they talk of love together.

ASCLEPIADES
[C. 129–40 B.C.]

EXPLANATIONS OF LOVE

There is a place where love begins and a place where
love ends.

There is a touch of two hands that foils all dictionaries.

There is a look of eyes fierce as a big Bethlehem open-
house furnace or a little green-eyed acetylene
torch.

There are single careless bywords portentous as the big
bend in the Mississippi River.

Hands, eyes, bywords—out of these love makes battle-
grounds and workshops.

There is a pair of shoes love wears and the coming is a
mystery.

There is a warning love sends and the cost of it is
never written till long afterward.

There are explanations of love in all languages and not
one found wiser than this:

There is a place where love begins and a place where
love ends—and love asks nothing.

CARL SANDBURG
[1878–1967]

INDEX
OF AUTHORS

INDEX OF FIRST LINES

ABOUT THE AUTHOR

Kathleen Blease has a degree in English literature and first served as an editor for two major publishing houses before starting out on her own as a freelance editor and writer. Over the span of her career, she has written on a variety of topics—from health to education to home improvements to parenthood—and edited books that have won acclaim throughout the country.

Seven years ago, her love unexpectedly knocked on her front door and introduced himself. She and Roger were married just three months later. Today, Kathleen is a stay-at-home mother of two small boys and a spare-time writer.

A collector of poetry and classic literature, Kathleen's first book, *Love in Verse: Classic Poems of the Heart,* is a Boston Book Review bestseller. Her other collections include *A Mother's Love: Classic Poems Celebrating the Maternal Heart, A Friend is Forever: Precious Poems that Celebrate the Beauty of Friendship, One Dark Night: 13 Masterpieces of the Macabre*, as well as several collections of quotes and prayers.

She lives with her husband and two children in the historic district of Easton, Pennsylvania.

SPECIAL DEDICATION

Sensual Love was in its early stages of production on September 11, 2001, when nearly 7,000 innocent civilians perished at the hands of terrorists. Thus, I would like to add this note.

My husband and I would like to express our sympathies to our fellow Americans who lost loved ones in New York City, Virginia, and Pennsylvania. We are deeply saddened by your loss, and you are remembered in our daily prayers.

To our other fellow citizens, I would like to make a special request:

By the time this book is off the press and in the bookstores, the events that took place on that September morning will seem, I pray, a bit distant. The images will have softened. We will have become accustomed to the hourly reports, the warnings and security measures, the prayers, the vigils, and hopes for peace to be renewed. We will have learned to live with how we have been changed, and our routines will have begun again.

Yet, I ask you, try to take time from your schedule to remember those we lost: the mothers and fathers, aunts and uncles, brothers and sisters, and our children and neighbors, each of whom helped make this nation a special place on earth. Remember, too, those who love and miss them.

Please dedicate a moment of peaceful reading to honor them.

Kathleen Blease
Easton, Pennsylvania

Printed in the United States
by Baker & Taylor Publisher Services